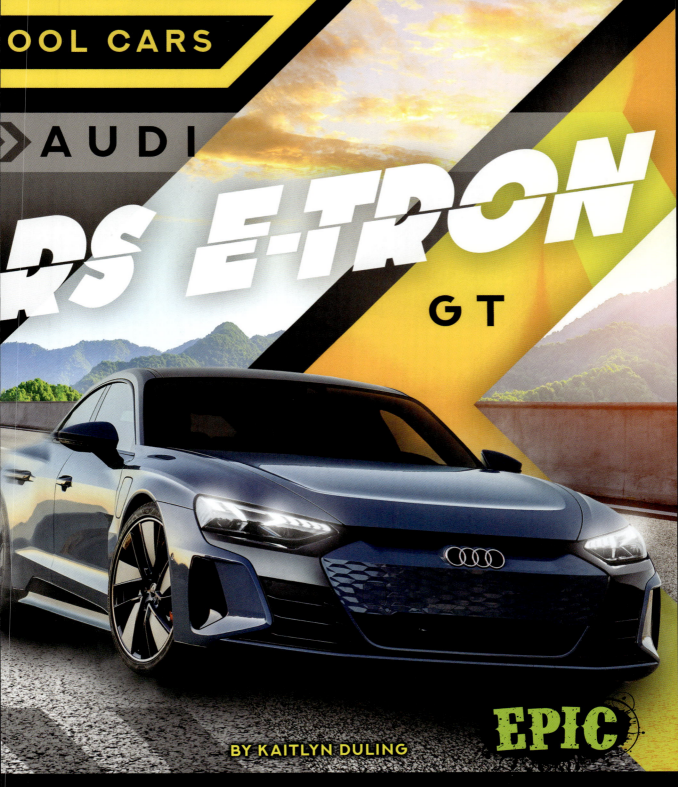

COOL CARS

AUDI RS E-TRON GT

BY KAITLYN DULING

BELLWETHER MEDIA ››› MINNEAPOLIS, MN

EPIC

EPIC BOOKS are no ordinary books. They burst with intense action, high-speed heroics, and shadows of the unknown. Are you ready for an Epic adventure?

This edition first published in 2024 by Bellwether Media, Inc.

No part of this publication may be reproduced in whole or in part without written permission of the publisher. For information regarding permission, write to Bellwether Media, Inc., Attention: Permissions Department, 6012 Blue Circle Drive, Minnetonka, MN 55343.

Library of Congress Cataloging-in-Publication Data

LC record for Audi RS e-tron GT available at: https://lccn.loc.gov/2023036107

Text copyright © 2024 by Bellwether Media, Inc. EPIC and associated logos are trademarks and/or registered trademarks of Bellwether Media, Inc.

Editor: Rachael Barnes   Designer: Jeffrey Kollock

Printed in the United States of America, North Mankato, MN.

TABLE OF CONTENTS

A GRAND ADVENTURE	4
ALL ABOUT THE RS E-TRON GT	6
PARTS OF THE RS E-TRON GT	12
THE RS E-TRON GT'S FUTURE	20
GLOSSARY	22
TO LEARN MORE	23
INDEX	24

A GRAND ADVENTURE

The Audi RS e-tron GT zips around corners. It speeds down straightaways. It grips the road.

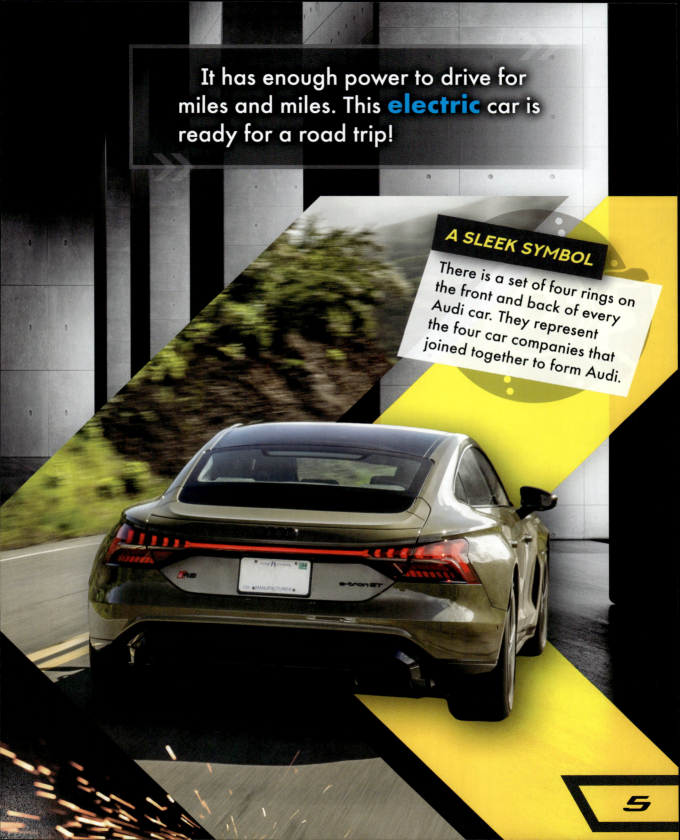

It has enough power to drive for miles and miles. This **electric** car is ready for a road trip!

A SLEEK SYMBOL

There is a set of four rings on the front and back of every Audi car. They represent the four car companies that joined together to form Audi.

ALL ABOUT THE RS E-TRON GT »

AUDI FACTORY AND OFFICES IN INGOLSTADT, GERMANY

AUGUST HORCH

August Horch founded Audi in 1909. Today, Audi makes **luxury** cars and motorcycles. The R8 and Quattro are famous car **models**.

Audi is based in Germany. But the company builds cars all over the world!

R8

📍 WHERE IS IT MADE?

EUROPE

INGOLSTADT, GERMANY

7

The RS e-tron GT was first made in 2021. The *GT* in its name stands for "grand touring." GT sports cars are made to drive long distances at top speeds.

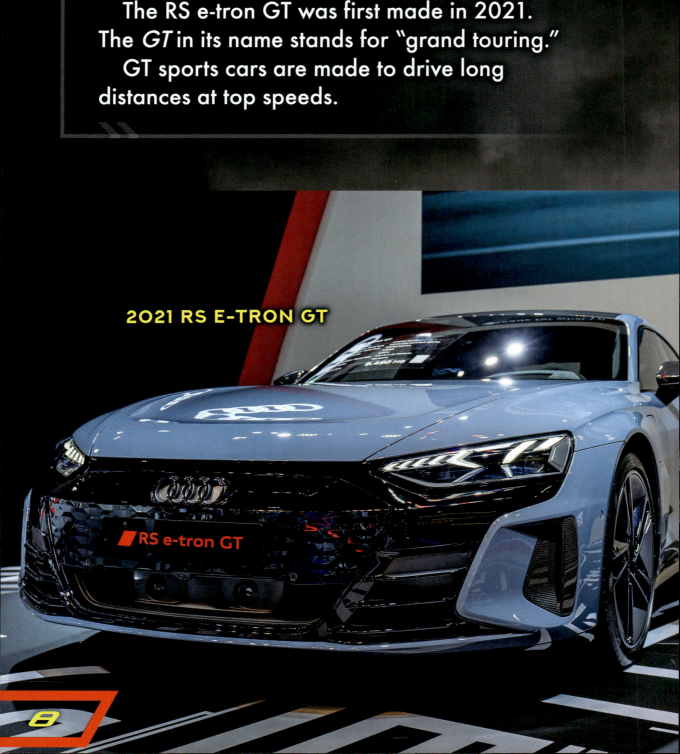

2021 RS E-TRON GT

⊛ RS E-TRON GT BASICS

YEAR FIRST MADE — 2021

COST — starts around $148,500

HOW MANY MADE — currently in production

FEATURES

dual electric motors

spoiler

fast charging port

The original Audi e-tron GT is fast. The RS model is even faster! *RS* means "racing sport."

The RS e-tron GT can reach 60 miles (97 kilometers) per hour in just 3.1 seconds!

PARTS OF THE RS E-TRON GT

The RS e-tron GT is run by two **electric motors**. They are powered by a **battery**. The car has two **charging ports**. A full battery can power the car for up to 293 miles (472 kilometers).

MOTOR SPECS

DUAL ELECTRIC MOTORS

TOP SPEED — 155 miles (249 kilometers) per hour

0-60 TIME — 3.1 seconds

HORSEPOWER — 637 hp

HEAR IT COMING

Electric cars have very quiet motors. To add excitement to the ride, Audi created different sounds for the RS e-tron GT. One sounds like a spaceship taking off!

The car's body is heavy and low to the ground. A **spoiler** pops up at high speeds. These features give the car strong **handling**.

SPOILER

SIZE CHART

WIDTH 77.3 inches (196.3 centimeters)

HEIGHT 55.4 inches (140.7 centimeters)

LENGTH 196.4 inches (498.9 centimeters)

15

Inside, the RS e-tron GT has luxury seats. Owners can choose front seats that give **massages**!

Drivers can turn on colored lights. The colors can be changed using the car's **touch screen**.

PLAN TO PLUG IN!
The RS e-tron GT's route planner shows nearby electric charging stations. Drivers can easily make plans to plug in and power up!

TOUCH SCREEN

17

Audi built a special model of this car. It is called the RS e-tron GT project _513/2.

RS E-TRON GT PROJECT _513/2

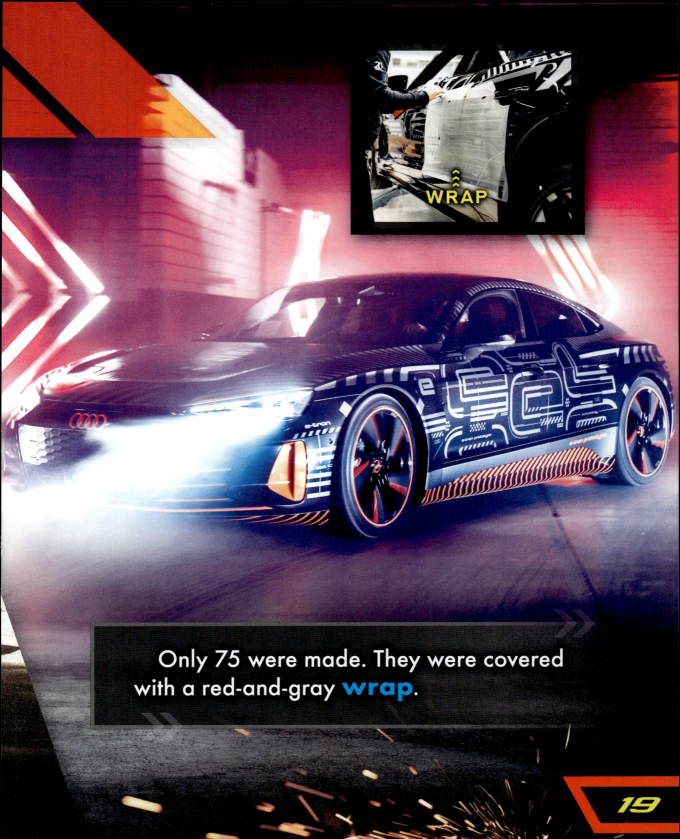

Only 75 were made. They were covered with a red-and-gray **wrap**.

THE RS E-TRON GT'S FUTURE »

Audi continues to make the RS e-tron GT. The 2024 model comes with **animated** lights! The company will build more electric cars. They also hope to produce safe **self-driving** cars. Audi's future is bright!

AUDI ELECTRIC CAR PRODUCTION

GLOSSARY

animated—appearing to move; animated lights flash and light up in different patterns.

battery—a part that supplies electric energy to a car

charging ports—openings that allow a charger to connect to an electric vehicle

electric—able to run without gasoline

electric motors—machines that give something the power to move by using electricity

handling—how a car performs around turns

luxury—having a high level of comfort

massages—treatment by pressing on a body part

models—specific kinds of cars

self-driving—able to travel without a human driver

spoiler—a part on the back of a car that helps the car grip the road

touch screen—a display on which people can select options by touching the screen

wrap—a special vinyl film on a car

TO LEARN MORE

AT THE LIBRARY

Adamson, Thomas K. *Porsche Taycan*. Minneapolis, Minn.: Bellwether Media, 2023.

Fenmore, Taylor. *Look Inside an Electric Car: How It Works*. Minneapolis, Minn.: Lerner Publications, 2024.

Greve, Meg. *Audi R8*. Minneapolis, Minn.: Kaleidoscope, 2022.

ON THE WEB

Factsurfer.com gives you a safe, fun way to find more information.

1. Go to www.factsurfer.com.

2. Enter "Audi RS e-tron GT" into the search box and click 🔍.

3. Select your book cover to see a list of related content.

INDEX

basics, 9
battery, 12
body, 14
charging ports, 12
charging stations, 17
colors, 17, 19
company, 5, 6, 7, 13, 18, 20
electric car, 5, 13, 20
electric motors, 12, 13
future, 20
Germany, 6, 7
handling, 14
history, 6, 8
Horch, August, 6
lights, 17, 20
models, 6, 7, 10, 18, 20
motor specs, 12
motorcycles, 6
name, 8, 10

number, 19
project_513/2, 18, 19
range, 5, 8, 12
rings, 5
seats, 16
self-driving cars, 20
size, 14–15
sounds, 13
speed, 4, 8, 10, 11, 14
spoiler, 14
touch screen, 17
wrap, 19

The images in this book are reproduced through the courtesy of: Audi, front cover, pp. 3, 4, 5, 7, 9 (isolated, motor, spoiler, port), 10, 11, 12, 13, 14 (main, spoiler), 15 (main, length), 16, 18, 19 (main, wrap), 20, 21; imageBROKER.com GmbH & Co. KG/ Alamy, p. 6; Eden78, p. 6 (August Horch); Supermop, p. 8; Mike Mareen, p. 14 (width); Gabo_Arts, p. 17.